Chri

B i b l e S t u d i e s

DECIDING WISELY

Bill Syrios

in 6 or 12 studies
for individuals or groups

With Notes for Leaders

INTERVARSITY PRESS
DOWNERS GROVE, ILLINOIS 60515

To my parents, Bill and Barbara Syrios,
who have provided considerable counsel, support and grace in all
my decisions . . . the good, the bad and the ugly.

InterVarsity Press is the book-publishing division of InterVarsity Christian Fellowship, a student movement active on campus at hundreds of universities, colleges and schools of nursing in the United States of America, and a member movement of the International Fellowship of Evangelical Students. For information about local and regional activities, write Public Relations Dept., InterVarsity Christian Fellowship, 6400 Schroeder Rd., P.O. Box 7895, Madison, WI 53707-7895.

All Scripture quotations, unless otherwise indicated, are taken from the HOLY BIBLE, NEW INTERNATIONAL VERSION. Copyright © 1973, 1978, 1984 International Bible Society. Used by permission of Zondervan Publishing House. All rights reserved.

Cover photograph: Robert McKendrick

ISBN 0-8308-1148-6

Printed in the United States of America ∞

17	16	15	14	13	12	11	10	9	8	7	6	5	4	3
05	04	03	02	01	00	99	98	97	96	95	94			

Contents

Welcome to Christian Character Bible Studies

What is a Christian character? And how does one go about developing it?

As with most questions of faith and the practice of faith, the best source of information is the Bible itself. The Christian Character Bible Studies explore a wide variety of biblical passages that speak of character development.

The Bible speaks of love—love for ourselves, love for God, love for other believers, and love for those who do not yet believe.

The Bible speaks of responsibility—responsibility for the poor, responsibility for the weak, responsibility for the environment, responsibility for our assets, responsibility to work and responsibility to share our faith.

The Bible speaks of holy living—honesty, sexual purity, mental discipline, faithfulness, courage and obedience.

The Bible speaks of hope—a hope that is based on the character of God, the work of Jesus Christ, and an accurate view of our human limitations. It is a hope that says, "Residence on earth is temporary; residence in heaven is eternal."

This series of Bible study guides will help you explore, in

thought and in practice, these many facets of Christian character. But why bother? Why can't we accept ourselves the way we are? Isn't that the route to mental health?

Not entirely. We are all in transition. Each new day brings new influences on who we are. We respond—and change. With God's help, that change can be toward Christian growth.

Growing in character is satisfying. It carries with it the sense of growing in godliness—into the image that God created us to be. It carries a sense of harmony, of walking hand in hand with God. But it is not painless. Therefore these guides will constantly ask us to hold up our character to the mirror of Scripture and to bend that character along the lines of Christ's image. God doesn't want us to stay the same. We should allow the Spirit to nudge us through these studies toward the spiritual maturity that God designed for his people.

What Kind of Guide Is This?

This is an inductive Bible study guide. That means that each study deals with a particular passage of Scripture and attempts to understand its content, its meaning, and its implications for godly living. A variety of questions will explore all three of those areas.

This is a thought-provoking guide. Each question assumes a variety of answers. Many questions do not have "right" answers, particularly questions that aim at meaning or application. Instead, the questions should inspire users to explore the passage in more depth.

This study guide is flexible—you can use it for individual study or in a group. You can vary the amount of time you take for each study, and you have various options for the number of studies you do from the guide. This is possible because every guide in this series is structured with two unique features. First, each of the six studies is divided into two parts, and second, several questions are marked with an asterisk (*), indicating that they may be

Guidelines for Using the Christian Character Bible Studies

Option	Type of Use	Time Allowed	Number of Sessions	Your Plan to Follow
1	Individual	30 minutes	12	Divide each study into two sessions, and use all the questions.
2	Individual	45 minutes	6	Use one study per session, and skip questions with an asterisk (*) if time doesn't allow for them.
3	Individual	60 minutes	6	Use one study per session, and use all the questions.
4	Group	30 minutes	12	Divide each study into two sessions, and skip questions with an asterisk(*) if time doesn't allow for them.
5	Group	45-60 minutes	12	Divide each study into two sessions, and use all the questions.
6	Group	60 minutes	6	Use one study per session, and skip questions with an asterisk (*) if time doesn't allow for them.
7	Group	90 minutes	6	Use one study per session, and use all the questions.

skipped if time does not allow for them. So you can have six sessions or twelve, with varying amounts of time to fit your needs.

How do you decide which approach is best for you? Looking at the chart on page 6, decide if you will be using this guide for individual study or in a group. Then determine how much time you want to spend on each session and how many sessions you want to have. Then follow the plan described in the far right column.

For example, if you are using this guide in a group, you can choose from options 4, 5, 6 or 7. If you have 45-60 minutes for study and discussion in each group meeting, then you can use option 5. Or if you have only 30 minutes available, you can use option 4. These options allow you to have twelve meetings by breaking at the dividing point in each session and using all the questions, including those with an asterisk.

If your group has only six meeting times available, then follow the column headed "Number of Sessions" down to options 6 and 7. Option 6 provides for 60-minute sessions without the asterisked questions while option 6 allows for 90-minute sessions using all the questions.

Note that there are four plans that allow for in-depth study— options 1, 3, 5 and 7. These use each of the questions and will allow for the most thorough examination of Scripture and of ourselves.

With seven different options available to you, Christian Character Bible Studies offer maximum flexibility to suit your schedule and needs.

Each study is composed of three sections: an introduction with a question of approach to the topic of the day, questions that invite study of the passage or passages, and leader's notes at the back of the book. The section of questions provides space for writing observations, either in preparation for the study or during the course of the discussion. This space can form a permanent record of your thoughts and spiritual progress.

Suggestions for Individual Study

1. Read the introduction. Consider the opening question, and make notes about your responses to it.

2. Pray, asking God to speak to you from his Word about this particular topic.

3. Read the passage in a modern translation of the Bible, marking phrases that seem important. Note in the margin any questions that come to your mind as you read.

4. Use the questions from the study guide to more thoroughly examine the passage. (Questions are phrased from the New International Version of the Bible.) Note your findings in the space provided. After you have made your own notes, read the corresponding leader's notes in the back of the book for further insights. (You can ignore the comments about moderating the dynamics of a discussion group.) Consult the bibliography for further information.

5. Re-read the entire passage, making further notes about its general principles and about the personal use you intend to make of them.

6. Pray. Speak to God about insights you have gained into his character—and your own. Tell him of any desires you have for specific growth. Ask his help as you attempt to live out the principles described in that passage.

Suggestions for Group Study

Joining a Bible study group can be a great avenue to spiritual growth. Here are a few guidelines that will help you as you participate in the studies in this guide.

1. These are inductive Bible studies. That means that you will discuss a particular passage of Scripture—in-depth. Only rarely should you refer to other portions of the Bible, and then only at the request of the leader. Of course, the Bible is internally consistent, and other good forms of study draw on that consistency, but inductive Bible study sticks with a single passage and works on it in-depth.

2. These are discussion studies. Questions in this guide aim at helping a group discuss together a passage of Scripture in order to understand its content, meaning and implications. Most people are either natural talkers or natural listeners. Yet this type of study works best if people participate more or less evenly. Try to curb any natural tendency to either excessive talking or excessive quiet. You and the rest of the group will benefit.

3. Most questions in this guide invite a variety of answers. If you disagree with someone else's comment, say so (kindly). Then explain your own point-of-view from the passage before you.

4. Be willing to lead a discussion. Much of the preparation for leading has already been accomplished in the writing of this guide. If you have observed someone else direct the discussion two or three times, you are probably ready to lead.

5. Respect the privacy of others in your group. Many people speak of things within the context of a Bible study/prayer group, that they do not want as public knowledge. Assume that personal information spoken within the group setting is private, unless you are specifically told otherwise. And don't talk about it elsewhere.

6. Enjoy your study. Prepare to grow. God bless.

Suggestions for Group Leaders

Specific suggestions to help you appear in the leader's notes at the back of this guide. Read the opening section of the leader's notes carefully, even if you are only leading one group meeting. Then you can go to the section on the particular study you will lead.

Introducing Deciding Wisely

Where should I go to college? The question plagued me for months as a young Christian close to graduation from high school. It finally boiled down to two universities in Kansas. One offered a small-college atmosphere and had a law school. (Law was an occupation I was considering.) The other was larger and offered a beautiful setting with lots of trees and a lake in the middle.

How could I decide? Would God guide me? How would he guide? I had made important decisions before but few which could shape my future as much as this choice.

In their helpful book, *Decision Making and the Will of God*, Gary Friesen and Robin Maxson offer two simple questions: "Is it moral? Is it wise?" These questions apply to every attempt to discern God's will.

But certain dilemmas persist. In non-moral decisions, like choosing a college, what is the wisest course of action?

After visiting both campuses, charting out the pros and cons, praying and talking to my parents and others in the Christian community, I still felt divided. Little did I know my choice would result in vocational change, an in-depth experience with Christian community and meeting my future wife. But I suspected just such things could happen!

Maybe I had two perfectly good choices and just needed to express gratefulness to God for his loving oversight and decide. . . .

Would he not "freely give me all good things" no matter which course I chose?

Decision day came. Everything being equal, one campus had a lot more trees and the other, newer buildings. I opted for the trees.

Which college, if any, should I attend? What vocation would be best to pursue? Where should I live? Who, if anyone, am I to marry? How can I most effectively counsel this person? What is the best way to spend my time? my energy? my money? Answering these kinds of questions amounts to a lifelong challenge. Though at times we struggle with whether God wants our best, often our struggle involves asking, "What exactly is the best that God wants?"

Jesus' promise to never leave us or forsake us applies in these day-to-day decisions. But in what way will his Spirit be present with us? Does he tell us what to do through impressions? or give signs? or use circumstances? To what extent should we lean on the counsel of others or our own intuition? And of course there is Scripture, prayer and the issue of obedience.

God will guide us. But how will he guide?

Principles for Deciding

This study guide is written with the following principles in mind:

1. God takes the initiative to work out *his sovereign will* in this world. We can relax, take courage and have peace.

2. The Scriptures provide the framework for *God's moral will*. As God's son or daughter, we are called to live within this framework.

3. God has no detailed plan beyond his moral will which he expects us to discover. We are not running a maze but have the responsibility and freedom to search out *godly wisdom* in making decisions.

4. *The Christian community* (and not inner feelings) is our greatest source of wisdom for working through the decision-making process. Western Christians in particular must resist the superficial voice of individualism and pursue the storehouse of wisdom found among God's people who are alive in his Spirit.

5. Finding God's will cannot be reduced to a three-point outline but is expanded to a lifetime *development of Godly character*. Wisdom is not so much found in "how to" guidance techniques but through pursuing the life we find with our creator, redeemer and friend.

Most of us find ourselves interested in the issue of God's will out of need—the need to make a particular decision among competing options. The typical dilemma of deciding between two options such as a college campus with beautiful trees or one with new buildings can be very difficult and very important to us. Be assured they are important to our Lord as well.

But he would have us use such decision making occasions to dig deeper, confronting who we are to be rather than fretting over how or where or with whom we are to be. Consequently, the studies in *Deciding Wisely* will burrow beneath the surface of everyday decisions to uncover the attitudes and character qualities upon which such decisions should be based.

For starters we need to ask, "Do I really want to *know* God's will?" And in the last study we'll consider the question, "Do I really want to *do* God's will?" In between we'll look at some case studies. Those studies highlight Jesus, Solomon, Moses, the psalmist and Paul as they wrestle with making wise decisions.

May you, in Paul's words, increasingly learn "to test and approve what God's will is—his good, pleasing and perfect will" (Rom 12:2).

Bill Syrios

ONE

DO I REALLY WANT TO KNOW GOD'S WILL?

John 5:1-15

A while back, I was talking to a real estate agent. He was giving me a sales pitch on why I ought to buy a house through him. He mentioned how his ability to listen to people's needs came out of a decade of being a professional counselor. I said, "Oh, really, you've been a counselor? Why did you decide to change professions?"

His answer surprised me. "Because people don't really want to change. At least in the real estate business I can see results. I like that."

Later, I asked another counselor what percentage of people she felt genuinely wanted to deal with the issue they were struggling with and were open to change. What percentage do you think she said?

"Maybe twenty per cent, more likely ten per cent."

Scott Peck begins his bestselling book *The Road Less Traveled* with a now famous understatement: "Life is difficult." He continues,

"Life is a series of problems. Do we want to moan about them or solve them? . . . [The] tendency to avoid problems and the emotional suffering inherent in them is the primary basis of all human mental illness."

Have you ever prayed, *"Lord, help me to want to want to want to change in this particular area"*? What a great prayer!

Finding God's will is a process which begins with a willingness, even a spark of willingness, to know that will. The desire to change, no matter how small, is a prelude for receiving the direction he wants for our lives.

Jesus constantly confronted people with the issue of personal change. In John 5:1-15 he encountered a man who was a prime candidate for change. The man was an invalid, probably paralyzed, for thirty-eight long years. His closest friends all consisted of social outcasts. His livelihood came from begging. His body was spent, his ego dragging, his future in grave doubt. . . . Enter Jesus.

Part One: Encounter with the Great Physician
1. What is one of the most difficult habits you've ever broken?

How did you change?

Read John 5:1-9a.
*2. The story occurs at a pool near the wall of Jerusalem. Why did the sick gather there?

3. What drew Jesus to this place?

4. Why do you think he chose this man for healing?

5. Why would Jesus ask the man if he wants to be healed?

*6. Why does the man answer in this way (v. 7)?

How would you describe the man's response?

7. Why might the invalid not want to be healed?

8. Why do you think Jesus healed the man in spite of his lack of faith?

*9. In what way do you identify with the invalid?

10. Have you ever been guilty of placing limitations on God's ability to bring positive change in your life? Explain.

Part Two: The Struggle to Embrace Health
*11. When did you last avoid doing something that would have been good for you?

Read John 5:9b-15.
*12. How do the Jews react to this obvious miracle?

*Why do you think they reacted in this way?

13. How would you contrast Jesus' concern for the man with that of the Jews?

14. Describe the man's response in verse 11.

15. In verse 14 Jesus warns the man to stop sinning. What sin do you think Jesus is referring to?

16. What are the benefits and costs of sinning for the man?

17. How does the man respond to Jesus' warning (v. 15)?

***18.** How could this action lead to a "worse thing"?

***19.** How could the man have responded in a healthy way to Jesus' warning?

20. What is an area of your life that if God asked, "Do you want to be healed?" you're not sure you'd say yes?

21. What would help you to be more open to the Lord in this area?

*optional question

TWO

PRAYING FOR
GOD'S WILL

Matthew 26:36-46; Matthew 6:5-15

I could see the question in my son's eyes before he even asked—
"Do I have to, Dad?"

Both of us felt awkward. I knew my request to take on the job
was appropriate. He did too. But his question seemed just as appropriate. It was a lot to ask a ten-year-old, and we both sensed the
need to stop and evaluate the cost versus benefits of the request.

Relationships built on mutual respect rarely demand blind obedience. And this is even more true of Jesus and his father who enjoy
complete trust between each other. But as the final hours before
the crucifixion approached, Jesus' grief about what lay ahead grew
intense. An awkward question came to mind, one though, that he
knew his father would help him to answer: *"Do I have to?"*

Implementing the Father's will, even for Jesus, was not just a
matter of putting his life on "automatic pilot." He, too, faced the
sometimes agonizing question as to whether he would make God's
will his will. What would be the costs? What would be the benefits?
Drawing on his Father's resources through prayer made all the
difference for him. It will for us as well.

Part One: "Not as I Will, but as You Will"
1. What's the most difficult thing you could imagine God wanting you to do?

Read Matthew 26:36-46.
2. What words or phrases are used to describe Jesus' mental state?

3. What concerns could threaten to overwhelm Jesus with sorrow?

4. Why do you think Jesus makes this unusual request of his Father in verse 39?

***5.** What is an issue or decision you have faced in which all the choices seemed to be hard ones? Explain.

6. What has characterized your prayers in such times of difficulty?

7. Why do you think Jesus chose to include Peter, James and John to accompany him at this time?

*8. How does Jesus express his frustration at their lack of support (vv. 40-41, 45-46)?

9. What is the significance of the progression between Jesus' prayer in verses 39 and 42?

*10. What is a situation you've faced in which persevering in prayer helped clarify God's will?

*11. What is a situation presently confronting you in which you want God's help to make a difficult decision to follow his will?

*Follow Jesus' example and seek out the support and encouragement of friends as you begin to struggle with that decision.

Part Two: "Your Will Be Done"
*12. If you could be assured that God would do one thing for you, what request would you make?

Read Matthew 6:5-15.
13. Contrast the reward received from hypocritical prayer versus genuine prayer (vv. 5-6).

*14. Why are "many words" unnecessary in our prayers (vv. 7-8)?

15. What is your greatest struggle with prayer?

16. How does Jesus' model prayer define who God is and who we are (vv. 9-13)?

17. What does it mean to ask that "your kingdom come, your will be done on earth as it is in heaven"?

18. Why is receiving God's forgiveness and offering forgiveness to others critical in knowing God and his will in our lives (vv. 12-15)?

19. How has prayer helped you to know God's will in a particular situation?

20. Spend time praying for concerns you have for God's will to be done.

*optional question

THREE

SEARCHING FOR GOD'S WISDOM

Psalm 119:1-24; 1 Corinthians 1:10—2:5

*F*ew situations bring life to a grinding halt like losing a contact lens. Have you ever seen it happen to a major league baseball pitcher? Frustration turns to comedy as fellow players trickle out from the dugout and hunch over the mound on hands and knees. Fans get restless. Commentators start reminiscing about recent games. The TV audience goes on commercial break.

If we are going to have the vision to see life from God's perspective, we will regularly have to stop everything, hunker down and find out just what that perspective is. Like finding a contact lens, God's wisdom is simply worth whatever inconveniences may come in its pursuit.

The Old and New Testaments give us our starting point in the search. These books provide us with the only inspired record of people's experience with their Creator and Redeemer. "All Scripture," Paul tells Timothy, "is God-breathed and useful for teaching, rebuking, correcting and training in righteousness" (2 Tim 3:16).

Psalm 119 highlights the expansive application of God's Word as it begins each stanza with a successive letter of the Hebrew alphabet. All of life's situations, everything from A to Z, find a transforming perspective in the light of that Word.

1 Corinthians highlights the radical contrast between the wisdom of God and the wisdom of man. "For the foolishness of God is wiser than man's wisdom, and the weakness of God is stronger than man's strength" (1 Cor 1:25). Our study of Psalm 119 and 1 Corinthians 1:10—2:5 will reaffirm to us the source and character of God's profound wisdom.

Part One: The ABC's of Knowing God's Will
1. What is a way the Bible has been helpful in your life?

Read Psalm 119:1-24.
*2. What different words does the psalmist use to describe God's Word?

3. In what ways does he communicate his commitment to Scripture?

*4. What benefits of knowing and following God's Word does the psalmist mention in verses 1-8?

5. How does God's Word help us to deal with sin (vv. 9-16)?

6. How does God's Word enlighten us about God's ways (vv. 17-24)?

*7. What are the consequences of *not* knowing or following God's Word (vv. 5-6, 9-11, 21-22)?

8. What is a way you have experienced frustration in studying Scripture?

9. What in the psalmist's example can bring encouragement to us to meditate on and delight in God's Word?

*10. What passage of Scripture is providing challenge or encouragement in your life right now?

*What is it teaching you about God?

Part Two: Wisdom from Above

*11. Describe something you perceived to be a certain way only to find out later it was just the opposite.

Read 1 Corinthians 1:18—2:5.

12. In what ways, according to Paul, is the world's wisdom at odds with God's wisdom (vv. 18-25)?

13. What kind of worldly wisdom seems to be prevalent among the people of Corinth?

14. What worldly thinking do you see as the strongest contender for the hearts and minds of people around you?

*15. How would the message of Christ be a stumbling block to the Jews?

*How is it foolishness to the Greeks?

16. What corrective does Paul bring to bear for the Corinthian Christians in his reminder of their life before Christ's call (vv. 26-31)?

17. In this context what does it mean to boast in the Lord?

18. Why is humility critical in helping us gain God's perspective?

19. How does Paul's ministry model the wisdom of God (2:1-5)?

*Read 1 Corinthians 1:10-17.
*20. How does the wisdom of Christ expose the worldliness of the Corinthians' power struggle?

*21. What would Paul say is the will of God for the Corinthian church?

22. How has the perspective brought by the gospel changed your understanding of God's will for your life?

*optional question

FOUR

MAKING GODLY CHOICES

1 Kings 3

One morning I decided to keep count of how many choices I made during the day. The experiment began after I woke up at 4:30 a.m. and tried to decide whether to get out of bed or to go back to sleep. So began choice number one. (Actually, it was number two since I had just decided to try the experiment.)

Subconscious routines became painfully conscious, like deciding (choice number five) how long to brush my teeth. Soon I decided (choice number eleven) to somehow distinguish between significant conscious choices and routine insignificant ones. But what would be the criteria for deciding between a significant and an insignificant choice?

The experiment was quickly breaking down. By breakfast time I was overwhelmed. So I chose to end the short-lived experiment (choice number fourteen). At that point I decided (choice number fifteen—oops, I decided to stop counting) to think about what I had learned.

Although the choices I had made were relatively insignificant, I could see that choices are like links in a chain. One inevitably leads to the next. Deciding to have orange juice for breakfast means I must then decide how much to pour.

Similarly, important decisions, whether wise or foolish, set up subsequent choices—a flow chart of sorts. If we start making wise choices, that course will likely lead to more wise choices. The same is true of foolish choices. Choosing, for instance, to live beyond our financial means will limit our subsequent options. Instead of being free from debt, we soon find ourselves making choices related to which creditor to pay and which to put off.

In the following story, we witness one of the greatest displays of wisdom from one of the wisest rulers in history—King Solomon. The famous dilemma regarding a baby claimed by two mothers is resolved, not from a stroke of luck, but from wise and godly decisions he previously made.

Part One: God-Given Opportunities

1. Describe a unique opportunity you were given which required you to make a choice.

What went into making your choice?

Read 1 Kings 3:1-15.

2. Solomon had just been established as king (see 2:46). How is the beginning of Solomon's reign described (vv. 1-4)?

*3. Why do you think God made the offer he did to Solomon in verse 5?

4. How would you describe Solomon's request in verse 9?

5. What guided Solomon in making his choice (vv. 6-9)?

6. Give an example in which you based—or failed to base—a decision on attitudes similar to Solomon's.

7. Why was God so pleased with Solomon's request (vv. 10-14)?

8. What significance do you find in God's abundant response to Solomon?

9. Wisdom involves much deeper issues in a person's life than the ability to make good decisions. How does this story show that wisdom is a character issue as well?

*10. Why is wisdom worth more than knowledge, money or power in our lives?

*11. What about Solomon's attitude would you like to apply in your own life? Explain.

Part Two: Making Good Decisions
*12. On a scale of 1 to 10 (1 being poor, 10 being excellent) how would you rate your ability to make good decisions? Explain.

Read 1 Kings 3:16-23.
13. What are the facts of the case up to this point?

*14. How would you describe Solomon's dilemma?

*15. What would you have done if you were faced with such a situation?

Read 1 Kings 3:24-28.
16. How do the women react to Solomon's order?

*17. Why do you think the one with the dead baby reacted as she did?

18. What risks did Solomon take with his rather unorthodox ruling?

19. Wisdom is sometimes characterized as cautious and deliberate. What decision have you recently faced that required a bold response? Explain.

20. How does this ruling publicly validate Solomon's encounter with God in verses 5-9 (see v. 28)?

*21. What is the significance of God's gift to Solomon for the nation of Israel?

22. Think of a decision in which you need wisdom. What do you want prayer for as you plan for this decision?

*optional question

FIVE

LEARNING TO LISTEN

Exodus 18:1-27; Acts 15:36—16:10

When I had the rare opportunity to preach in a church of a cultural background distinct from my own, I was determined to fit in. So I "revved up" my intonations to a feverous pitch. From the front right pew a dear lady, Mrs. Johnson, waved me on with her hanky and "amens" aplenty. My topic was grace.

"So," I began my conclusion, "do you believe God helps those who help themselves?" I asked, expecting a "no"—if any answer at all.

"Amen. Y - E - S!" shouted Mrs. Johnson.

"Well I don't," I blurted out.

"NO, NO, NO!" Mrs. Johnson quickly agreed.

Most likely a murky message from me contributed to her faulty answer, but what came to my mind in post-sermon ruminations was Mrs. Johnson's selective perception. I could certainly identify with that because I often don't really listen to people. Instead, I find myself "amen-ing" them with a perfunctory "uh-huh" while silently waiting to jump in with my own thoughts. Can you relate?

But good listening is more than an art. It is a spiritual issue. "Thus says the Lord," intoned the Old Testament prophets with the implied question, "Is anyone listening?" "He who has ears to hear," Jesus repeatedly encouraged, "let him hear."

Christian maturity deepens as we realize that God's guidance is not primarily intuitive. That is, it does not originate from feelings within us. Rather, it comes from the Holy Spirit working through God's Word and his people who love us enough not to leave us to our own devices. This study provides a model of individuals who resisted the temptation of "amen-ing" the voice of God by listening with their decision-making process on the line.

Part One: Openness to Others

1. From whom are you least likely to seek advice? Why?

*Read Exodus 18:1-12.

*2. How is the meeting between Jethro and Moses described (vv. 1-7)?

*3. How did Jethro respond to Moses' enthusiastic description of what God had done for Israel (vv. 8-12)?

Read Exodus 18:13-27.

4. How would you characterize Jethro's advice to Moses for handling disputes among the people (vv. 17-23)?

5. What were the potential pros and cons of Jethro's advice?

6. Why might it have been difficult for Moses to follow Jethro's advice?

*7. Do you find it difficult to respond to feedback or criticism? Explain.

How have you found it important to listen to such feedback?

8. Why do you think Moses listened to Jethro and followed his advice (vv. 24-26)?

9. What do you think the results of these changes meant to the people?

to Moses?

10. How can you be more open to the counsel and critical feedback of others?

How does, or could, such feedback benefit you?

Part Two: Openness to the Spirit
*11. Do you find yourself trusting in or skeptical of supernatural experiences believers claim to have? Explain.

Read Acts 15:36—16:10.
12. During their first missionary journey, John Mark leaves Paul and Barnabas and returns to Jerusalem (Acts 13:13). Why do you think Paul is reluctant to give him a second chance?

*13. How would you expect Barnabas to argue for his position?

14. Do you think the disagreement between Paul and Barnabas was worth separating over? Explain.

*15. When is it legitimate or not legitimate to break ranks with a fellow Christian?

16. What actions does Paul take in 16:1-5 and why?

*17. What actions does the Holy Spirit take in 16:6-10?

18. The text is unclear regarding the two communications of the Spirit in verses 6 and 7. However, in verse 9 Paul has a vision. What do you think gave Paul confidence that these experiences were accurate indicators of the Spirit's direction?

*19. Why might it have been critical for God to intervene supernaturally in this situation?

*20. Have you ever had such a clearcut supernatural encounter with the Lord? Explain.

21. What is the difference between the decision-making process employed elsewhere in this passage and the one employed here (16:6-10)?

22. What are the drawbacks of depending on our feelings as accurate indicators of the Lord's direction for us?

23. What is a decision about which you would appreciate (or know you need) counsel from others in the Christian community?

*optional question

SIX

DO I REALLY WANT TO DO GOD'S WILL?

John 9:1-41

*A*friend of mine named Roger was traveling alone through a remote area of Guatemala and decided to explore what is one of the largest caves in the world. For the trip in he took a flashlight and two candles.

Roger was deep into the cave when his flashlight began to dim. Turning back to retrace his steps, he came to a sheer wall. He thought he had memorized his pathway in but became disoriented on his way back by the cave's intricate web of chambers. Countless minutes were lost as Roger retraced his steps, now running and stumbling as he held the dim flashlight low to the ground.

After his flashlight batteries went dead, he lit his first candle and then his second. With the second and last candle down to half its size, he was no closer to finding his way out. For the next few hours he sat down in utter darkness, reflected on his life, shivered, cried and prayed. The agony of dying alone in a remote cave grew even more intense as he realized his parents would never find out what happened to him.

With his half a candle, Roger took the last-chance risk of going still deeper into the cave to re-examine one of his turns. There he noticed a footprint which he had missed before and, as the last candle gave out, he began to see a faint glimmer of grayness that marked the direction to the cave's entrance.

Most likely the value of light is something Roger will never un-derestimate. His plight resembled the blind man of John 9 who had only one last chance to find his way out of the darkness.

"While I am in the world," Jesus told that man, "I am the light of the world." Our study will help remind us how critical the light of Jesus is to our own well-being.

Part One: Telling the Truth
1. Have you ever shaded the truth or told a lie that came back to haunt you? Describe the situation.

Read John 9:1-12.
2. What does the disciples' question in verse 2 reveal about their understanding of sin and its consequences?

3. What is Jesus' perspective concerning the man's condition (vv. 3-5)?

*4. How does Jesus' declaration in verse 5 become a practical reality for the blind man (vv. 6-12)?

*5. How do his neighbors respond?

Read John 9:13-23.
6. What concerns prompt the Pharisees' interrogation of the man?

7. What do you think blocks them from being truly open to Jesus and his ministry (v. 16)?

*8. When do you resist hearing and responding to the truth?

9. In verses 18-23 the man's parents become involved. What do they risk in confirming their son's story?

*10. What are common situations in which fear of rejection stops people from standing up for someone or for telling the truth?

*11. Are you sometimes intimidated or unduly influenced by other people's strong opinions or actions? Explain.

12. What is a difficult situation you find yourself in which requires being guided by the truth?

Part Two: Living the Truth
*13. Have you initially judged someone only to later change your mind entirely about that person? Describe the situation.

Read John 9:24-41.
14. During the second interrogation of the formerly blind man (vv. 24-34), the Pharisees reveal some of their biases against Jesus. How does the man turn the tables and challenge them?

*15. Are his brutal honesty and sarcasm appropriate? Explain.

16. Why are the Pharisees so offended by this man's healing?

*17. What role do the Pharisees play in helping the man grow in his understanding of Jesus?

18. What are the consequences of the man's truthfulness?

How does Jesus reward the man's faithfulness to the truth in verses 35-38?

19. Think of a specific way Jesus has brought the light of his truth into your life. Describe how embracing this truth has had both negative and positive consequences for you.

*20. How does Jesus define his mission in this world (vv. 39-41)?

How does it relate to being the light of the world (v. 5)?

21. Verse 31 reminds us that God "listens to the godly man (or woman) who does his will." What does it mean to do God's will according to this story?

22. Finding God's will is often the easy part—at least when you compare it to doing his will. In what way has your study of God's will challenged your understanding or commitment to his will?

*optional question

Leader's Notes

Leading a Bible discussion can be an enjoyable and rewarding experience. But it can also be intimidating—especially if you've never done it before. If this is how you feel, you're in good company. When God asked Moses to lead the Israelites out of Egypt, he replied, "O Lord, please send someone else to do it!" (Ex 4:13). But God's response to all of his servants—including you—is essentially the same: "My grace is sufficient for you" (2 Cor 12:9).

There is another reason you should feel encouraged. Leading a Bible discussion is not difficult if you follow certain guidelines. You don't need to be an expert on the Bible or a trained teacher. The suggestions listed below should enable you to effectively and enjoyably fulfill your role as leader. And remember the discussion leader usually learns the most—so lead and grow!

Preparing for the Study

Group leaders can prepare to lead a group by following much the same pattern outlined for individual study at the beginning of this guide. Try to begin preparation far enough in advance for the Spirit of God to begin to use the passage in your own life. Then you will have some idea about what group members will experience as they attempt to live out the passage. Advance preparation will also give your mind time to thoughtfully consider the concepts—probably in odd moments when you least expect it.

Study the flow of the questions. Consider the time available. Plan for an appropriate break (if you are using two sessions) and which optional questions you will use. Note this in your study guide so that you will not feel lost in the middle of the discussion. But be ready to make changes "en route" if the pattern of discussion demands it. Pencil near the questions any information from the leader's section that you don't want to forget. This will eliminate clumsy page turns in the middle of the discussion.

And pray. Pray for each person in the group—by name. Ask that God will prepare that person, just as he is preparing you, to confront the truths of this passage of his Word.

During the Study

1. One of the major jobs of the discussion leader is to pace the study. Don't make your job more difficult by beginning late. So keep an eye on the clock. When the

agreed time to begin arrives, launch the study.

2. Take appropriate note of the introductory essay, then ask the approach question. Encourage each of the group members to respond to the question. When everyone is involved in discussing the general topic of the day, you are ready to explore the Scripture.

3. Read the passage aloud, or ask others to read aloud—by paragraphs, not verses. Verse-by-verse reading breaks the flow of thought and reduces understanding. And silent reading often makes concentration difficult, especially for people who are distracted by small noises or who are uncomfortable with group silence. So read aloud—by paragraphs.

4. Keep in mind that the leader's job is to help a group to discover together the content, meaning and implications of a passage of Scripture. People should focus on each other and on the Bible—not necessarily on you. Your job is to moderate a discussion, to keep conversation from lagging, to draw in quiet members, and to pace the study. So encourage multiple responses to questions, and encourage people to interact with each other's observations. Volunteer your own answers only in similar proportion to others in the group.

5. Pacing is a major difficulty for inexperienced leaders. Most group participants have set obligations after a scheduled Bible study. You will earn their thanks if you close the study at a predictable time. But to do so you don't want to race ahead and miss details in the early questions; nor do you want to play catch-up at the end: skipping sections people most want to talk about. Try writing in your study guide the time that you hope to finish questions at various points in the study. This will help you keep a steady pace. Note also any optional questions that you can add or subtract, depending on the pace of the study. But be alert to particular needs and interests in the group. Sometimes you should abandon even the best-laid plans in order to tend to these.

6. If possible, spend time talking about personal needs and praying together. Many groups begin or end by speaking of various worries, concerns, reasons for thanksgiving—or just their plans for the week. Groups who pray together often see God at work in ways far beyond their expectations. It's an excellent way to grow in faith.

7. If you have time, do some further reading on small groups and the dynamics of such groups. For a short, but helpful, overview read *Leading Bible Discussions* by James Nyquist and Jack Kuhatschek (InterVarsity Press). Or for a more in-depth discussion read *Small Group Leaders' Handbook* or *Good Things Come in Small Groups*, both of which are edited by Ron Nicholas (InterVarsity Press). For an excellent study of how small groups can contribute to spiritual growth read *Pilgrims in Progress* by Jim and Carol Plueddemann (Harold Shaw).

The following notes refer to specific studies in the guide:

Study 1. Do I Really Want to Know God's Will? John 5:1-15.

Purpose: To highlight why we would want to pursue knowing God's will even though it may involve difficult change for us.

General Note: You should be familiar with the introduction of *Deciding Wisely* at the front of this guide. It would be helpful to point out the principles for deciding in the introduction to your group.

Although there are some differences of opinion in the Christian community regarding how the Lord guides his people, this guide seeks to delve beneath "how to" principles. The passages chosen to study will help explore the foundation God's will and wisdom provide for our decision making.

Question 1. The purpose of this specific question is to raise the issue of personal change. Such an exercise should help the group identify how hard it can be to reverse directions and adopt new patterns of life.

Question 2. John is very specific about the location of this healing. Though there is now some question about its exact location, most commentators place it just north of the Temple area. Have those in the group with a map of Jerusalem in the back of their Bible find where the Sheep Gate and pool are. Then have someone point out their location so everyone can have a look.

Some ancient manuscripts add verse 4 which explains an apparent legend about why the sick congregated here—because an angel would periodically stir the water, and the first one in would be cured. While this may very well explain the presence of the people and this invalid in particular (see v. 7), the best manuscripts of the original text omit verse 4. The stirring waters were more likely caused by intermittent bubbling from an underground spring.

Question 3. Help people in your group get a feel for the scene. The pool area is the equivalent of a first-century outdoor hospital but with no nurses, no doctors and no medicine. The place must have reeked of death. What drew Jesus to this place was not the superstition of angelic healing, but the people who were desperate for hope and help.

Question 4. It's not surprising that Jesus shows up here, but what he does turns out to be quite intriguing. Of those present his choice may be directed toward the most disabled of the disabled, the one who had been there the longest and whose condition, the most hopeless. Surely the person he focuses on qualified for such status.

For thirty-eight years this man had lived with what appears to be, from verse 8, a condition of paralysis. The number of years may have symbolic significance to John as well. "The man who had waited," to quote John Marsh, "for his hope to be fulfilled for thirty-eight years was in the precise situation of his people long ago when they wandered and waited for thirty-eight years (Deut 2:14) for the promise of God to be fulfilled to them" (*The Gospel of St. John*, p. 250). As such, the man's condition represented the larger paralysis of Israel who desperately needed the restoring power of God.

Question 5. Verses 6-7 are central to the story. What would you expect Jesus to ask the man? This is a question you could ask the group before you ask question 5. I would have expected Jesus to ask a question such as, "Could you have faith in One who is sent from God?" But faith is never mentioned during this entire story. His actual question is unexpectedly straightforward: "Do you want to get well?" Push your group to see the unusual nature of such a question: What kind of question is this? Why would Jesus call for such a simplistic response?

Question 6. You might ask a follow-up question to 6b such as: "Does the man's answer sound a bit canned?" You would expect the man to say something like, "Of course I want to get well!" Instead it's almost as if this man had rehearsed over and over in his mind the two-sentence response (v. 7) of why he was forever doomed to his condition. Maybe Jesus asked the question because he knew the man could not even conceive of being healed. Thirty-eight years of paralysis had likely produced a lot of frustration and anger, a lot of hopelessness and self-pity. Being healed was nowhere near a realistic possibility.

Or just maybe Jesus asked the question, "Do you want to get well?" because he suspected the man really didn't want to get well. It hadn't been a great life for this man, but it was his life—a known quantity. And besides, thirty-eight years qualified him as the biggest beggar on the block. What that profession took away in self-esteem, it gave back in hard cold cash.

Question 8. Though faith in the Gospels is often a prerequisite to healing, it is not here. You may want to draw out some discussion concerning the fact that Jesus is not limited by human response in his work.

Instead of faith, Jesus finds in the man only self-pity and a commitment to live on his own terms. "What gives God the right to mess with my life?" is an appropriate rhetorical question. The concrete of self-determination had hardened solid. Jesus gets out the jackhammer of his mercy and totally messes with this guy's life through an unexpected and unmerited healing.

But the healing is also an act of judgment, because it once and for all dismantles any potential for self-righteous bitterness. Now the man had absolutely no excuse when God would ask him (as he likely would again), "Do you want to get well?"

Questions 9-10. Jesus' question begs the question for us: "Do we really want to get well?" Certainly Jesus is willing to change us . . . to give us discipline, self-control, self-assurance, empathy for others, a spirit of generosity. But are we willing participants—are we open to him and to each other, or are we simply realistic thinkers, comfortable to try and get by?

Personally, I am prepared to admit each and every problem that I can handle. But a willingness to change starts with admitting, or maybe even more foundationally just recognizing, there are all kinds of problems I cannot handle. The difference, as John Piper states in *Desiring God*, between Uncle Sam and Jesus Christ is that Uncle Sam won't enlist you unless you are well, and Jesus Christ won't enlist you unless you are sick. "It is not the healthy who need a doctor," said Jesus, "but the sick. I have not come to call the righteous, but sinners" (Mk 2:17).

Question 12. If you are studying the passage in two parts, then you will want to read 5:1-15 to refresh your memory and to include anyone who missed the first part.

Questions 14-17. The invalid of John 5 was a self-protective man. Jesus' gracious work in his life fell on an unresponsive heart. In time, as he reflected on how God had healed the pain in his body, he might be ready to open up the pain in his soul. Maybe he would one day come to know Jesus as the Great Physician of both body and of soul. But that day had not yet come. In verses 10-15 we see the consequences of his failure to take Jesus seriously.

The hostile response of the Jewish leaders (v. 10) is the first example of their resistance to Jesus in John's Gospel. But the man is similarly resistant: "He replied [to the Jews], 'The man who made me well [he doesn't know Jesus' name] said to me, "Pick up your mat and walk" ' " (v. 11). It's like he's saying, "I didn't mean to get healed; it's not my fault I'm carrying my mat. This fellow who healed me told me to do it. It's his [Jesus] fault I was healed." Later, in verse 15, he even goes out of his way to specifically betray Jesus as the "guilty party" to his adversaries. (You might want to note that the results of the man's betrayal was the persecution that followed in verses 16-18.)

The man has become a victim of Jesus' healing! How ironic. A lifestyle of self-protection had so distorted his perspective that he ends up blaming Jesus instead of thanking him.

Self-protection and love are opposites. If love is the ultimate virtue, self-protection is the ultimate sin.

Question 18. Verse 14 implies that the man continued to hold on to his sin. Jesus' warning to stop sinning is a call to repent and be reconciled to God. The spiritual fate of eternal alienation would be a far worse consequence than any physical handicap.

Question 19. A follow-up question here could be, "What might repentance have involved for this man?"

Questions 20-21. You might review the study's introduction for this question. Responding to Jesus by making real changes starts with the realization that it will be *more difficult* to change than to stay the same. However, if we stay motivated in the difficult process of change, though hard initially, it will ultimately lead to real faith, hope and love. And the opposite is also true—resistance to change will end up leading one to unbelief, hopelessness and selfishness.

Study 2. Praying for God's Will. Matthew 26:36-46; Matthew 6:5-15.

Purpose: To incorporate Jesus' example of dependence on the Father in our decision making.

Question 1. If you think this question is too "heavy" for your group modify it by asking, "What is *one of* the most difficult things you could imagine God wanting you to do?"

Question 2. Introduce this question with some background. Jesus has just finished supper with his disciples in the upper room. He predicted Peter's denial (26:31-35) and now proceeds to the Mount of Olives, a quiet spot to which Luke says he was accustomed to going. The peacefulness of the location just east of Jerusalem gave little clue as to the monumental drama which was about to take place.

Question 3. Jesus experiences severe anguish here. Three times he prays in deep emotional distress. Now he must face the purpose for his coming to earth. His death, however, would not be like some of his followers who would willingly suffer martyrdom in the centuries to come. They would face death in the strength of God's presence. Instead, as D. A. Carson says, "Jesus went to his death knowing that it was his Father's will that he face death completely alone (27:46) as the sacrificial, wrath-averting Passover Lamb. As his death was unique, so also his anguish, and our best response to it is hushed worship."

Question 4. You could initially ask, "What is unique about Jesus' prayer in v. 39?" Never before in the Gospel has there been any obvious hesitation on Jesus' part. Even in his confrontation with Satan (4:1-11) there was no sense of doubt. But now he must face not only suffering and death but also the "cup" which includes God's wrath for sin. It may be that Jesus simply did not know if any other way was possible. But likely he knew only too well that he was to experience being cut off from his Father as he took on the sins of the world (see 27:46).

Question 6. If you use question 5, this question is a natural follow-up and can be made more specific, "What characterized your prayers during this time of difficulty?"

Questions 7-8. Because Jesus' anguish is unique, his prayer is personal. But the disciples, who have accompanied him for three years, have the opportunity to provide Jesus with the strength of their presence. The opportunity, however, is lost as they repeatedly fall asleep.

Jesus' concern is that his disciples not "fall into temptation" (v. 41). Falling asleep betrayed the lack of resolve that led to their defection (v. 56), a defection which he predicted in verses 31-35 and which Peter carried through with dismal precision in verses 69-75. Even in his own great pain, Jesus is aware of trials that his disciples will themselves face. He speaks compassionately, yet truthfully about temptation: "The spirit is willing, but the body is weak" (v. 41).

Question 9. The progression seems to be one of clarity and resolve. In the prayer of verse 39, Jesus asks for the cup to be taken—if possible. In verse 42 he does not ask for the cup to be taken away, only for his Father's will to be done.

Questions 10-11. Note that these are both application questions. Question 10 focuses on the past and question 11 on the present. Encourage group members to be as concrete and specific as possible in their sharing. You may want to share first in order to model such specificity. If you have enough time, go around the circle so each one can answer question 11 or break the group into twos or threes for sharing and prayer.

Question 12. If you are making this a separate study, go around the circle and have each group member respond. If you feel like it would help, first ask for "one request from your wildest imagination." Then go around again asking for a serious request.

Question 13. Note that reward is the consequence of prayer according to Jesus. If it is done to impress others, our reward is simply that—a reputation for piety. If, however, prayer is done with God's blessing in mind, another reward naturally follows—the power of his presence and help. Prayer provides us the opportunity to join in intimate partnership with our Creator and Redeemer. As Martin Luther said, "Prayer is not overcoming God's reluctance but laying hold of his highest willingness."

If time allows, it would prove thought-provoking to ask: "Why do we pray? For God's sake or for our own sake?" Since God knows our needs better than we do (v. 8), it is clear that prayer is for us. Through prayer, we cast off self-sufficiency and place our dependence on him. Prayer helps clarify that in every situation true reward comes only from knowing and following Jesus.

Question 15. Many commentators point out that verses 5-6 warn against devotional practices prevalent among the Jews—hypocritical prayer, and verses 7-8 warn against those of the Gentiles—meaningless repetitive prayer. While the distinction may not be completely clear-cut, such an explanation could be a good introduction for question 15 which focuses on our particular struggles in prayer.

Question 16. In contrast to the ostentatious or thoughtless prayer practices of others, Jesus gives his disciples a model, or maybe better, the right frame of mind for prayer. This question should allow the group to thoroughly investigate Jesus' prayer. Make sure you give them plenty of time with it. The prayer focuses on God as the all-sufficient Provider and us as the all-deficient recipients.

Question 17. Praying "your kingdom come, your will be done" is a prayer of commitment. This prayer commits God's people to hallow his name in accordance with the values of his kingdom and the purposes of his will. The phrase "on earth as it is in heaven" expresses a heartfelt desire for the outworking of God's reign within this world's order. You can tie in Jesus' prayer in Gethsemane (part one of this study) here by pointing out the consistency of his desire to see God's will being done.

Question 18. Reconciliation is central to Jesus' prayer as it is central to the gospel itself. Unreconciled relationships will stand in the way of knowing and doing God's will. Matthew 5:23-24 makes it even clearer that unreconciled relationships are cause for "stopping everything" to see that forgiveness and acceptance are brought to bear. Applying God's grace goes a long way in clarifying how we are to live with one another.

Question 20. You could begin this question by asking your group to write down five areas of concerns. Then they can pick one or two in which to pray about. People with similar concerns could also be placed together if you break the group up in threes or fours to pray.

Study 3. Searching for God's Wisdom. Psalm 119:1-24; 1 Corinthians 1:10—2:5.
Purpose: To anchor our search for wisdom in the Word and wisdom of God.
Question 2. Psalm 119, the longest in the book of Psalms, is so full of appreciation for God's Word that only three verses (vv. 84, 121 and 122) make no reference to

it. That Word is alternately described as God's law, his statutes, precepts, testimonies, ordinances, commandments and promises.

As the introduction points out, this psalm is an alphabetic acrostic psalm. Each Hebrew letter of its 22-letter alphabet introduces eight successive verses. It is the A-to-Z description of Scripture's sufficiency as our guide to God's will. You can introduce your study by saying you will be studying the literal "ABC's"—or in Hebrew the *aleph, beth, gimel's*—of commitment to God's will!

Question 3. The psalmist may very well be the young man referred to in verse 9. His "journal," beginning in verse 5, is filled with personal pronouns. As such it is not an exhortation to study God's Word, but rather personal reflections and prayers on its excellency and practicality in his own life. If he is preaching to us, it comes through the vehicle of example. His delight (vv. 16, 24) for God's Word betrays an affection for God that has spoiled him from anything the world has to offer.

Questions 4-6. These questions are meant to introduce the group to each section of the study (vv. 1-8, 9-16 and 17-24). Use them to help your group get an overview. Don't move too quickly through them, however. After initial observations, and if you anticipate time will allow, ask follow-up questions that help the group delve deeper such as: "What verbs does the psalmist use which describe his feelings for God's Word? What does his use of all the personal pronouns communicate?" etc.

Questions 8-9. It is hard not to feel inspired by the joy in God's Word expressed by the psalmist. Our own experience with studying Scripture, however, can fall far short of his experience. Remember his "journal" is not meant to produce guilt but to express the pleasure he has found. Question 8 should help the group honestly face the struggles we all have studying Scripture. Such honesty will open us to the example of the psalmist and to the encouragement of each other to press on in our pursuit of God through his Word.

Question 10. If you have extra time, you might want to substitute the following assignment for question 10: Have each member in the group (individually or in pairs) pick one other section from Psalm 119 and read it. Then ask, "What does this section say about knowing God through his Word?" Share the conclusions with the group.

If you are concluding the study with this question, encourage the group to pray to God as the psalmist did: "Open my eyes that I may see wonderful things in your law" (Ps 119:18).

Question 11. Be ready to get the discussion going by giving your own specific answer for this approach question as an example to the group.

Question 12. If you are studying both passages in one study, a helpful transition would explain that 1 Corinthians provides a stark contrast between God-centered wisdom and human-centered wisdom. This passage offers a case study of applying the mind of God to a practical problem: church division. Some background on the Corinthian church is in order.

The Greeks coined a word for leading a life of debauchery: *Korinthiazein;* that is, "to live like a Corinthian." Corinth was home to a cult dedicated to the glorification of sex. One thousand temple prostitutes worked their trade from the Temple of Aphrodite, the Greek goddess of love. Not far away at the Temple of Apollo, the god of ideal male beauty, the workers promoted homosexual practices.

You might have someone in the group point out on a map where Corinth was located. As a seaport of a quarter million people, Corinth's commercial and strategic importance to the Roman government led to increasing prosperity. Its cosmopolitan character included Romans, Greeks and Phoenicians and a sizeable Jewish community. Philosophers, bureaucrats, merchants, sailors, slaves and hucksters made Corinth a tough, brash metropolis not unlike a San Francisco, Rio de Janeiro or Tokyo of today.

Paul's initial ministry in Corinth lasted about eighteen months from approximately March 50 to September 51 AD (Acts 18:1-18). After rough treatment at the hands of the Macedonians, especially at Phillipi, and a less than spectacular response in Athens, Paul found many in Corinth ready to hear the good news. By the time Paul left with Aquila and Priscilla, he could look back with praise to God for his faithfulness and with affection for many new brothers and sisters.

Question 13. It is understandable that when Paul, now in Ephesus, heard of church division from Chloe's household (1 Cor 1:11), he set pen to paper to correct the factious spirit.

Old ways of thinking held a powerful temptation for the Corinthian Christians. Once they had each followed their own favorite philosopher. Now they were again aligning themselves, only to new leaders—some to Paul, others to Apollos and still others to Cephas (1 Cor 1:12). Such separation led to quarrels about who was right rather than unity in the life-changing message of the cross. Simple love of the brethren must not be replaced for the worldly exaltation of intellect and power.

Instead of a mere admonishment, Paul promotes unity by delving deeply into the profound wisdom of God. Paul's words here offer penetrating insight into who God is and how he carries on his work. The application of Paul's message originally gives a basis for healing division in the church (which is left for questions 20-21), but the implications of "how God thinks" touches every area of life.

Question 14. Help your group to be as specific as possible. If necessary, ask follow-up questions focusing on different subgroups—business or university cultures, social networks, even the church—which are influenced by worldly thinking.

Question 15. Paul divides the world into Jews and Greeks. They represent different points of contention with the message of the cross. Jews matter-of-factly demand practical evidence of God's power, and a crucified Messiah was a contradiction in terms. Greeks proudly pursue speculative philosophy, and Christianity's message offers their debates little in mystical other-worldly truth. Crucifixion to the Jews was an offense and to the Greeks, stupidity. But to those who are called, it is something very different: the power and wisdom of God.

Questions 17-18. If there is one quality absolutely critical to deciding wisely, it is humility. A humble spirit looks to God for wisdom and when found gives the credit where credit is due. Feel free to spend plenty of time in discussion of question 18.

Questions 20-21. It is important that the group clearly sees what originally prompted Paul to make such a stark contrast between godly and worldly thinking—disunity among the Corinthian Christians. Rivalry among Christians contradicts the gospel's message of reconciliation.

Question 22. Paul's argument in 1:18—2:5 is meant to provide a basis for reconciled relationships within the Christian community. It is those very relationships that will provide us with a great deal of input concerning God's will for our life. We will focus on this issue in study 5.

God's wisdom brought to bear on the whole of our Christian life will have significant implications. This question should help the group explore some of those implications.

Study 4. Making Godly Choices. 1 Kings 3.

Purpose: To identify attitudes that foster godly wisdom for decision making.

Question 1. This question offers the group an opportunity to get to know some of each other's history. If you are making part one a separate study, you may want to take the time to go around the circle, giving each person an opportunity to share.

Question 2. Solomon's reign begins with a considerable show of dedication to God. The law forbade marriage to peoples who lived in Israel such as the Canaanites (Ex 34:16; Deut 7:3), and his marriage to foreign wives led him to compromise his faith in Yahweh in his old age (see 1 Kings 11:1-8).

Solomon's marriage to Pharaoh's daughter (3:1), however, does not appear to be a breach of commitment. She is excluded from the wives that led him into worship of other gods (1 Kings 11:1). In fact, according to Jewish tradition, she became a follower of Yahweh herself. Marriage to an Egyptian brought Israel into a political alliance with its southern neighbor, adding to the security of Solomon's kingdom. But all was not totally well. The people had no central place of worship. This led them to sacrificing at mounds around the countryside called "high places" (1 Kings 3:2), the most important being at Gibeon (3:4). Since worship at high places was common in the Canaanite religion, Israel was strictly forbidden to use pagan altars (see Deut 12:1-14). Israel's history is checkered with repeated compromise to its neighbor's pagan beliefs by such practices. But there were a number of high places consecrated to the worship of Yahweh. Here the practice is excused as a matter of necessity since "a temple had not yet been built for the Name of the Lord" (1 Kings 3:2).

The author describes Solomon's love for God as similar to his father David, a man after God's own heart (3:3). What seems to qualify Solomon's godliness—the "except" in verse 3—"may in actuality not be intended to detract from his character. It may well be that both here and in v. 2 the statement concerning worshiping in various high places is an allusion to a state of incompleteness that did not end until the temple was completed" (*The Expositor's Bible Commentary*, p. 44). Reflecting his thankfulness and desire for God's blessing on his reign, Solomon offers the Lord a great sacrifice of a thousand burnt offerings at Gibeon.

Question 3. It is characteristic of God's grace that he would choose as king the one least likely: in this case the son of a once scandalous relationship between David and Bathsheba. Solomon is very aware of God's "great kindness" (3:6). He also is aware of his own inadequacy (3:7), not the least being his youth of under twenty years. God's compassion and power surrounded this young king from day one. This is evident in God's openness to Solomon: "Ask for whatever you want me to give you" (3:5).

Question 4. You could begin by asking: "If you were given Solomon's opportunity, for what would you have asked? Be honest!"

Question 5. Solomon shows maturity beyond his years in his request in verse 9. Note his clear self-understanding as an unmerited heir of God's grace through his father David and his role as a "servant," a word repeated four times (vv. 6-9).

Feel free to ask follow-up questions to help the group see the significance of Solomon's self-understanding. As a lead-in to question 6, you could ask, "Who has impressed you with a kind of humility similar to Solomon's?"

Questions 7-8. Rejecting the smaller ambitions of wealth, a long life and victory over his enemies, Solomon provides an apt illustration of Matthew 6:33: "Seek first his kingdom and his righteousness, and all these things will be given to you as well." In light of this you could ask, "How is Solomon's request and God's response an illustration of Matthew 6:33?" To get a description of the wisdom God gave Solomon, have someone in your group read 1 Kings 4:29-34. To get an idea of the extent of Solomon's wealth, fame and achievements see 1 Kings 10:1-29.

Question 9. This question is meant to help the group "nail down" the fact that wisdom is a character trait more than a decision-making issue. At its heart, wisdom is more than just having common sense. Its opposite—foolishness—is likewise not just a lack of common sense but something morally worse: a lack of common-sense lifestyle.

For this reason *Deciding Wisely* comfortably fits in a series on Christian character. The question of decision making is not so much a matter whether I should choose option A or B, but upon what attitudes and character qualities these everyday decisions are based. Such a perspective on wisdom will sharpen the way we interpret Scripture's perspective on wisdom.

Take James 1:5 for example: "If any of you lacks wisdom, he should ask God who gives generously to all without finding fault, and it will be given to him." Many read this verse as a promise of God's help in making a decision. But if wisdom is more of a character issue than a decision-making issue, what James is encouraging is much more than a request for insight on whether to do A or B. Instead he is calling for a humble, maturing approach toward God that looks to him for growth in the kind of character on which quality decisions stand. James 1:2-4, with its emphasis on finding joy in trials and developing perseverance in our faith, makes the fact that wisdom is a character issue even clearer.

Thus the writer of Proverbs declares, "The fear of the Lord is the beginning of wisdom" (Prov 9:10). Wisdom develops as we, like Solomon, understand our place as humble recipients of God's kindness, and his place as the all-sufficient One who, as James says, "gives generously to all."

Question 10. Knowledge, money and power may get us what we want. But true wisdom is evidence that God is working in our lives to give us what we need.

Question 11. If you are concluding the study with this question, you might want to wrap up the study by reading the celebration of wisdom found in Proverbs 8:1-21 and then praying together.

Question 13. If you are doing part two as a separate study, it would be helpful, before reading 1 Kings 3:16-23, to have someone who has studied part one give a summary of Solomon's request for wisdom (1 Kings 3:1-15).

Question 14. This story well illustrates the depth of Solomon's wisdom. The dilemma posed by the conflicting testimonies may not seem so difficult to us since we know how Solomon solved the case. But cases with no independent eyewitnesses, and where the testimony is one person's word against another, can prove extremely hard to judge fairly. You might want to point out a modern-day example.

Question 15. Even though most people will know Solomon's solution, press the group to think of how they would try to handle this dilemma. You might ask if there are some not familiar with Solomon's solution and if they would answer first.

Question 17. Besides the desire to mother a child, the mother of the dead baby apparently was filled with envy toward the other woman. So if she could not have the live baby, she didn't want the real mother to have the opportunity denied her.

Question 18. In ordering that the baby be cut in half, Solomon takes a calculated risk. What kind of reputation would Solomon have gotten if neither woman spoke up, and they both went home with half a baby?!

Question 19. Some may consider the exercise of wisdom a conservative no-risks approach to living, but such is not the case (as illustrated here). You may want to go around the circle to give each group member an opportunity to respond to this question.

Question 21. Unfortunately, later in life Solomon may have grown so secure in his gift that his faith turned presumptuous, leading him to the worship of other gods—a most unwise choice! This situation tragically played itself out in the actions of his son and successor Rehoboam (see 1 Kings 12). During much of Solomon's life, however, God's gift to him proved a great blessing to the entire nation.

Question 22. If time permits, you could close by reading the call to wisdom found in Proverbs 9:1-12 and praying.

Study 5. Learning to Listen. Exodus 18:1-27; Acts 15:36—16:10.

Purpose: To develop openness to the Holy Spirit's direction through the counsel of others.

Question 1. If it seems awkward to specify a particular person for this question, direct the group to identify from what kind of person it is difficult to seek advice.

Question 2. The book of Exodus describes God's deliverance of the Israelites from the cruel bondage of life in Egypt. In their trek through the desert, the people prove ungrateful and rebellious yet God patiently provides for their needs. The young nation and their leader, Moses, have much to learn about their God.

News of Israel's deliverance from Egypt undoubtedly traveled fast among the desert nomads of Sinai. In chapter 18 Moses receives a visit from his father-in-law, Jethro, at "the mountain of God" (either Mt. Horeb or Mt. Sinai). Jethro brings with him Moses' wife, Zipporah, and sons Gershom and Eliezer. The numerous repetition of Jethro's kinship with Moses in this chapter lends an air of an ancient neareastern family reunion. The greeting between the two men (vv. 5-8) reflects one of mutual respect and family affection.

Question 3. Jethro's visit also gives him an opportunity to satisfy his curiosity about what God had done for the Israelites. As a priest, and probably the chief priest, of the Midianites (18:1), Jethro shared a familiarity with Moses' faith in Yahweh since he, too, is a descendent of Abraham, through the line of Midian (Gen 25:2).

It is unclear whether Jethro joins in worship (18:12) as a new convert to faith in Yahweh or if he had previously known and worshipped Yahweh as the One "greater than all other gods" (v. 11). Either way, Jethro is caught up in Moses' enthusiasm for God's obvious involvement with the people Moses is leading, and it appears he vows commitment to the God who is leading Moses.

Question 4. You may want to note for the group that Jethro starts with a question (v. 14). Then you could ask how this would soften any defensiveness Moses might have to Jethro's advice. Moses' response indicates his concern as a leader to insure justice among God's people. His crucial oversight involves a teaching (v. 15) and a judicial (v. 16) ministry.

Jethro shares Moses' concern and suggests Moses remain involved as a representative for the people before God (v. 19) and as a practical interpreter of God's Word to the people (v. 20). But now the judicial load should be supplemented by capable, trustworthy, God-fearing, honest men (v. 21). Such decentralization reflects military organization that makes perfect sense. It just takes someone not so intimately involved to highlight an obvious problem and the common-sense solution.

Ask follow-up questions if necessary for the group to see Jethro's humble acknowledgement of the need for God's involvement in any plan (see vv. 19 and 23). His advice, though full of conviction, is "easy to hear" because his attitude is characterized by humility and a desire for the welfare of others, particularly Moses.

Questions 5-6. There are potential pitfalls in Jethro's suggestions. Any time responsibility is delegated, there is a loss of control by the leader. Will those who hear the people's cases judge justly and wisely? Surely Moses must have felt anxious to delegate leadership. Press your group to discuss how and why it might have been difficult for him to pass on his responsibility, including the fact that he would not be as needed in a diminished leadership role. Could he be struggling with pride and power, or was he just overly conscientious and anxious?

Question 7. Discussing issues Moses faced in delegation will provide a natural transition into the struggles (highlighted by question 7) that we face in listening to others and making changes in the way we do things.

Question 8. Moses' openness to Jethro gives further validity for his description in Numbers 12:3 as the humblest person on earth. It is likely that the judicial decisions made here were later codified into the kind of practical principles of desert living found in Exodus 21:1—23:13.

The story of Exodus 18 comfortably joins God's will as revealed by divine communication to his prophet (Moses) and God's will as discovered in the wisdom of human experience (Jethro). This is even more remarkable when we note the source of the human wisdom: a Midianite who does not share in the commonwealth of Israel.

Question 9. You might ask, "What could the long hours of work do to Moses' ability to judge?" And further, "What can happen when justice is delayed?" Moses recognized that implementing Jethro's plan would actually insure the continued dissemination of wise judgment. Thus we see God's will for him as the one who would still judge the most difficult cases and for the people who could rely on a capable and expeditious court system.

Question 10. This focus can hardly be overemphasized in a culture that encourages individualism as its primary value. Humility toward God will also be expressed toward one another as we give each other real access to our thinking and permission to be actively involved in our decision-making process.

Question 12. Acts 15 recounts the momentous events of the council of Jerusalem. The council, including key leaders such as Paul, Peter and James, convened to address whether Gentiles, who were becoming Christians by the hundreds, should be required to obey Jewish law. The verdict was that Gentile Christians should exercise cultural sensitivity and restraint to ease Jewish conscience, but the adequacy of the gospel rested on Jesus alone.

Upon hearing the news, the church in Antioch, which included many Gentiles, responded with great joy (Acts 15:30-35). The gospel was now "officially" freed from the cultural trappings of its Jewish heritage. In the shadow of this resounding show of unity, Acts' author, Luke, now turns his attention to a sad story of division.

Acts 15:36 records the beginning of Paul's second missionary journey intended to retrace the apostle's first trip in southern Asia Minor. It would be helpful to have someone in the group point out Paul's first missionary journey on a map in the back of their Bible. (It is recorded in Acts 13—14.)

During the first trip, Paul's companions included his trusted friend Barnabas and Barnabas' cousin John Mark. Soon after that trip began, Mark, for reasons that remain unclear, left and returned to Jerusalem (Acts 13:13). Possibly he was not prepared for the rigors of evangelism with Paul. Whatever it was, Paul felt Mark's departure was unjustified and would not consider the inclusion of a deserter in this new venture.

Question 13. Since Mark was Barnabas' cousin, he may have felt particular responsibility to see the young man mature. Most likely Barnabas, true to his name as "son of encouragement," saw promise in Mark and championed him (as he had done for Paul in Acts 9:26-27) for a second chance.

Question 14. Luke does not gloss over Paul's and Barnabas' "sharp disagreement," and the two form separate missionary expeditions. Barnabas takes Mark and returns to his native Cyprus while Paul takes Silas and returns to his native Anatolia. Although it could be reasonably argued that the arrangement fostered twice the evangelism, "this example of God's providence," as John Stott says, "may not be used as an excuse for Christian quarrelling."

Question 15. Jesus places great value on unity among his followers as reflected in his prayer in John 17 (especially v. 11). In John 17:20-21 Jesus anticipates that unity among Christians will act as a testimony to the world of his validity. The apostles saw in Jesus God's destruction of the "dividing wall of hostility" (Eph 2:14). His supernatural power could even unite those who were once enemies—the first-century Jews and Gentiles. Time and time again the church is called to unity, the kind it had magnificently experienced at the council of Jerusalem.

But human nature wars against such unity, and there are numerous examples of Christians in conflict with one another (for example, 1 Cor 1:10; Phil 4:2-3; James 4:1-2, 11). It is certainly legitimate to "agree to disagree," but Paul's and Barnabas' conflict became contentious. (The Greek word translated as "sharp disagreement" in 15:39 is very strong.) The message of reconciliation, which Paul so powerfully articulated, ultimately softened the apostle himself as he welcomed Mark back as a worthy brother (see Col 4:10; Philem 23; and especially 2 Tim 4:11).

When is it legitimate for a Christian to separate himself or herself from other Christians? This question has plagued the church since its inception. Given the New Testament emphasis, any separation must be thought through with the utmost care and caution. Just like divorce between spouses is not God's will, "divorce" among believers is not God's will.

The essentials of the faith must be at stake before Christians break fellowship. Of course, the questions then arise: "What are the essentials? What is an issue of doctrine, lifestyle or philosophy of ministry that is so critical that I would deem it legitimate to separate myself from other Christians?" My inclination is that we are quick to make essentials out of what, in final analysis, are non-essentials. These questions could make good follow-up questions for group discussion.

Question 16. Paul chose to add Timothy as a traveling companion, perhaps as a substitute for John Mark. As an uncircumcised half-Jew (on his mother's side), Timothy's presence could have provoked needless opposition from local Jews. But his circumcision seems to contradict the freedom from Jewish religious practices which the gospel embodied and which the Jerusalem counsel had recently validated. Certainly this is what Paul taught and fought for, especially against the Judaizers (Acts

15:1-2; Gal 1—6).

But Paul also recognized that once the principle that circumcision was not necessary for salvation was firmly established, he could make concessions in certain cases in order to further his Great Commission passion: "To the Jews I became like a Jew, to win the Jews" (1 Cor 9:20).

It is helpful to recognize that in making the decision to circumcise Timothy, Paul had to weigh two critical principles: The supercultural freedom of the gospel and cultural sensitivity for effective evangelism. You might want to ask the group: "What issues did Paul have to weigh in making his surprising decision to circumcise Timothy?"

Question 17. Note where Bithynia (to the north) and Macedonia (to the west) are on a map. It is speculative as to why the Holy Spirit stopped Paul's natural inclination to continue north (16:7), furthering the evangelization of Asia Minor, and instead turned him west. But his entrance into Macedonia establishes the first recorded evidence of the gospel reaching European soil. Such an expansion continues to fulfill Jesus' call: "You will be my witnesses in Jerusalem, and in all Judea and Samaria, and to the ends of the earth" (Acts 1:7). And it brings them ever closer to confronting the power source of the known world—Rome.

Questions 18-19. Paul charted out a specific plan as indicated by 15:36. He wanted to retrace his previous steps to strengthen those who became believers during his first visit. Paul's redirection, at least the one described in verse 9, comes from an intervention of the Holy Spirit in the form of a vision. Apparently it was so important for Paul to change his plans that God used a supernatural event to get his attention.

Since the text gives little detail, these questions are necessarily speculative in nature. They are meant to help your group discuss how God communicates his will. There very well may be differences of opinion in your group. Feel free to allow group members the freedom to state those opinions but encourage them to support their positions.

Question 21. Note that up to this point Paul has made a number of decisions, including the choice to (1) make this second journey (15:36), (2) include Barnabas (v. 36), (3) not take Mark (v. 38), (4) go north through Syria and Cilicia (v. 41), (5) take Timothy along, and (6) circumcise him (16:3). The criteria for these decisions was that Paul did or did not "think it wise" (15:38). (His initial decision not to take Mark was likely a wise one except that he then appears unwilling to re-evaluate it fairly under Barnabas' prompting.)

The above examples of employing godly wisdom are the most typical means of guidance throughout Acts. In Acts 16:6-10, however, the decision-making process makes a significant change to direct supernatural guidance. It is the untypical nature of such guidance that gives Luke (who has just joined Paul as evidenced by the "we" in v. 10) reason to highlight it.

Question 22. The Lord's direct guidance, such as Acts 16:6-10, would have the same moral imperative as the revelatory guidance of Scripture. Such a concrete experience goes far beyond a subjective feeling characterized by what is sometimes referred to as an "inner prompting of the Spirit." Such promptings must be stamped with the label *subjective* and open to careful evaluation.

This is not to say inner impressions are not legitimate factors in sizing up one's options when making a decision. Certainly they help us understand our own desire or lack of desire. But given our own sinful capacity to see only what we want to see, inner impressions must be open to the scrutiny and feedback of others, particularly others in the Christian community.

Question 23. You can personalize this question for your group if you would like: "What is a decision you are presently facing for which we (or some of us) could provide helpful counsel?"

Study 6. Do I Really Want to Do God's Will? John 9:1-41.

Purpose: To grow in our commitment to hear the truth and live in its light.

Question 2. The rabbis of the day debated whether and how a person's present physical condition resulted from a prior spiritual condition. Two interpretations emerged which are expressed in the disciples' question in verse 2 of whether the man's blindness resulted from his sin or from his parents' sin.

Question 3. Jesus attempts no such link between past events and present suffering, rejecting both popular alternatives. Jesus' explanation, "this happened so that" (v. 3), suggests a cause of the man's blindness and Jesus' healing which illustrates God's work. The connection states, in effect, that the issue is not some past transgression but the present opportunity to display the power of God. When Jesus shows up, the past is of no account. People will be made whole. God will be glorified.

Question 4. You may want to begin by asking the group, "Can you think of anyone else in the Bible who healed someone of blindness?" Then you can relate that Old Testament prophets and New Testament apostles exercised the gift of miracles on a number of occasions. But there is not one example in the Old Testament of someone receiving their sight. And likewise there are no examples in the New Testament of the apostles healing someone from blindness.

As far as we know Jesus is the only person in the history of humankind who has healed someone from blindness. And in this particular case, not only was the man blind, he was *born* blind. Giving sight to the blind is an absolutely unique miracle. He wasn't kidding when he said, "I am the light of the world."

Some have seen in Jesus' use of clay an act akin to God's creation of man from the dust mixed by moisture in Genesis 2:5-7. This connection identifies Jesus as God's instrument of re-creation, putting aright the created order which has been marred by human sin. The reason Jesus directs the man to wash in the pool of Siloam (which means "sent") appears to have significance as well. Jesus, the "sent one from the Father," now sends the one who would soon become his disciple to the "waters of baptism," giving him a new identification with Jesus.

Question 5. The man, who is now also identified as a beggar, returns to his home seeing. You may want to note that Jesus' healing will allow the man to change vocations, restoring not only his sight but his self-respect in the community as well.

The neighbors, who are apparently divided between those who knew him well and those who had "formerly seen him begging" (v. 8), were astonished and perplexed. Some even questioned whether this man was in fact the blind beggar. The man puts an end to the speculation by asserting, "I am the man" (v. 9).

Question 6. Some kind of interrogation by the religious authorities is to be expected. Again there is a division of opinion, but this time the focus is on Jesus. His actions violate two Jewish laws in doing a work of healing and in kneading the clay with spittle and dust on the sabbath.

In the Gospels it almost seems that Jesus purposely makes the sabbath his primary day of healing. If time permits, you might want to ask your group, "Why would Jesus heal on the sabbath? Does it seem to add any additional significance to the event?" He very well may have wanted to confront the incorrect sabbath understanding promoted by the religious establishment. But even more likely, instead of picking the most inappropriate day, he spontaneously chooses the most appropriate day to celebrate the re-creative work of God and bring joy into his world.

The more doctrinally minded Pharisees start with the sabbath violation and form the opinion that Jesus cannot be from God. The more open-minded start with the miracle and state their dilemma: "How can a sinner do such miraculous signs?" (v. 16). Their attention then turns to the man whose years of begging must have helped him develop a straightforward personality: "He is a prophet," the man declares when the Pharisees question him about Jesus.

Wrong answer! At least equating Jesus to a person uniquely gifted as a prophet was not an answer the Pharisees could accept. So they turn their attention to the parents.

Question 9. The intimidating questioning of the parents by the Pharisees brings a threat of expulsion from the synagogue as verse 22 makes clear. Such an act of excommunication, if actually carried out, would effectively cut the man's parents' relational ties to their community and possibly even their spiritual connections with God. The man's parents are not prepared to risk confrontation with the authorities and avow their ignorance of the Healer's identity. They are very careful to offer only the facts that the former blind man is indeed their son and to state that he is "of age" (over 13 years old) so he can bear valid testimony.

Questions 11-12. These questions should help people identify guiding forces in their lives. How much are we influenced by the opinions and actions of others (good and bad) and how much by our own sense of the truth in a situation? As time permits, ask group members to relate specific incidents in their lives which provide examples of this struggle. If people cannot come up with a present situation for question 12, backtrack by referring to the past, "What *has been* a difficult situation you found yourself in which required being guided by the truth." You may want to share first in order to provide a model of specificity.

Question 14. If you are studying the passage in two parts, then you will want to have 9:1-41 read aloud to refresh your memory and to include anyone who missed the first part.

Evidently the Pharisees have made up their minds which of the two views that previously divided them is true—Jesus has broken the sabbath and is thus a sinner. They make a demand to the man, "Give glory to God" (v. 24) which is actually a solemn directive: *We charge you to tell the truth.* "We know this man is a sinner. . . . What did he do to you? How did he open your eyes?" (vv. 24, 26).

The man's answer is characteristically straightforward: "One thing I do know. I was blind but now I see" (v. 25). His simple testimony of a changed life continues throughout the centuries to be the unshakable experiential evidence of Jesus' power, confounding the most stringent of critics.

Question 15. The former blind man is one colorful individual! His tenacity provides a contrast with his timid parents and an even greater contrast to the invalid who was healed by Jesus in John 5 (the first study). At this point you might want to remind the group of your first study.

The stories of the two men in John 5 and John 9, both healed on the sabbath, act as bookends to this guide. The invalid in John 5 ends up "blaming" Jesus for his healing, apparently because it challenged him with the uncomfortable issue of change, not to mention ruining his career of begging. The issue study one brought up is summarized in Jesus' question to that man: "Do you want to get well?" An encounter with Jesus necessarily brings to light our need for openness to the transforming power of Jesus in our lives. The response of the man in John 9 is very different. He knows his blindness is more than just a physical condition, and he opens up his spiritual need to the Great Physician as well.

Question 16. What brings the man closer to Jesus drives the Pharisees further and further away. They have made their choice and identify themselves as followers of an "old Moses" of the Law, a law more fundamentally of their own making. Now the "new Moses" has arrived, full of grace and truth (Jn 1:14; see also Mt 5:21, 27), but they will only boast of being the representatives of old Israel. Their only defense: "as for this fellow [Jesus], we don't even know where he comes from" (v. 29).

Such a defense actually contradicted what the people had said at the feast of Tabernacles (Jn 7:27). But to quote John Marsh, "The contradiction is purely formal. Both sayings are instances of John's irony, being both false and true together. The authorities do know Jesus' birthplace, though they do not know his divine origin; so any statement of ignorance or knowledge about Jesus' origins on their lips will be both true and false. This is the awful fate of those who reject the light that shines to reveal things in their reality" (*The Gospel of St. John,* p. 385). In effect, the Pharisees have taken a bite of the truth, but with that they are satisfied and ignore any further hunger pangs—quite a pity now that the full feast is set before them.

Question 17. The Pharisees have "progressed" from the view that Jesus is "not from

God" (v. 16), to questioning the miracle (v. 18), then speaking of Jesus as "a sinner" (v. 24), showing their ignorance (v. 29) and finally having themselves characterized by Jesus as guilty sinners (v. 41). The man, on the other hand, begins by referring to Jesus as a man (v. 11), to seeing him as a prophet (v. 17). Now he willingly acknowledges allegiance to Jesus as a worthy consideration (v. 27) and that Jesus is a man "from God" (v. 33). Finally in verses 35-38, he commits to Jesus his own allegiance in worship.

Question 18. What the parents feared, the man must endure. No Israelite would now have anything to do with him. Of course, he is now part of a new Israel. His excommunication, the most severe punishment short of capital punishment, constitutes the first experience of persecution suffered by a disciple of Jesus. But Jesus hears about what happens and searches him out.

The man's suffering, however severe, pales in significance to the gift of Jesus' light now illuminating his life. For now the Lord has given him double vision; he sees not only with his eyes but also with his heart. Such is the nature of suffering in the kingdom of God. The only thing more sacrificial than following Jesus is not following him.

Question 19. Encourage the group to be as specific and concrete in their sharing as possible. If time allows, go around the circle so each one can share briefly. Another possibility is to break the group down into threes or fours for a time of sharing on this question.

Question 20. Jesus sums up his mission in verse 39. When the Light of the world enters the darkness, blind men end up seeing, and seeing men end up blind. Given their opposition, the Pharisees must have expected Jesus to label them as blind. But he says blindness would give them an excuse. Instead they claim to see but refuse to believe their eyes. Their condition is thus not one of blindness but of guilt.

Question 21. This question concludes this study. The man in John 9 is the only man in the Gospel accounts for whom it explicitly says he worshipped Jesus. Surely this man models for us someone who follows the truth to its logical conclusion and commits his life to new realities as they increasingly become clear.

Question 22. This question concludes the guide as a whole. If time permits, ask the group to look back over the guide and the passages it highlights for a few minutes, and then ask this question.

End your time by praying for each other that God's will would increasingly be affirmed in your desire to open your life to the Light of the world.

Bill Syrios and his wife, Teresa, live with their boys, Luke, Andrew, Phillip and Mark, in Eugene, Oregon. Bill operates a real estate investment business and works with Inter-Varsity Christian Fellowship at the University of Oregon.

For Further Reading

Bonhoeffer, Dietrich. *Life Together*. San Francisco: Harper and Row, 1976.

Crabb, Larry. *Inside Out*. Colorado Springs, Colo.: NavPress, 1988.

Douglas, J. D. *The New Bible Dictionary*. Grand Rapids, Mich.: Eerdmans, 1962.

Ferguson, Sinclair. *Discovering God's Will*. Edinburgh, Scotland: Banner of Truth Trust, 1982.

Friesen, Gary, and Robin Maxson. *Decison Making and the Will of God*. Portland, Ore.: Multnomah, 1985.

Nicholas, Ron, et. al. *Good Things Come in Small Groups*. Downers Grove, Ill.: InterVarsity Press, 1985.

Nyquist, James, and Jack Kuhatschek. *Leading Bible Discussions*. Downers Grove: InterVarsity Press, 1985.

Peterson, Eugene. *A Long Obedience in the Same Direction*. Downers Grove, Ill.: InterVarsity Press, 1980.

Piper, John. *Desiring God*. Portland, Ore.: Multnomah, 1986.

Piper, John. *The Pleasures of God*. Portland, Ore.: Multnomah, 1991.

Plueddemann, Jim and Carol. *Pilgrims in Progress*. Wheaton: Harold Shaw, 1990.

Smith, Blaine. *Knowing God's Will*. Rev. ed. Downers Grove, Ill.: InterVarsity Press, 1991.

White, John. *Magnificent Obsession*. Downers Grove, Ill.: InterVarsity Press, rev. 1990.

Christian Character Bible Studies from InterVarsity Press
in 6 or 12 studies for individuals or groups

Deciding Wisely by Bill Syrios. Making tough decisions is part of life. Through these Bible studies, you'll find out how to pray for God's will, listen to his voice and become a wise person. These principles of godly decision-making will enable you to serve God in the decisions you make. 1148-6.

Finding Contentment by Carolyn Nystrom. The contentment that character-izes the Christian life is found in intangibles—trust, love, joy, comfort and hope. The studies in this guide will introduce you to these keys to complete fulfillment in Christ. 1145-1.

Living in the World by Carolyn Nystrom. How do we glorify God in secular work? How should we spend our money? What kind of political involvement should we have? This guide is designed to help us clarify godly values so that we will not be affected by the warped values of the world. 1144-3.

Loving God by Carolyn Nystrom. Studies on how God loves—and how his gracious and stubborn love provide the foundation for our love for him. As we learn to love God as he loves us, we'll learn how to be more who he wants us to be. 1141-9.

Loving One Another by Carolyn Nystrom. This guide will help you to solve your differences with other Christians, learn to worship together, encourage one another and open up to each other. Discover the bond of love between believers that is a joyful tie! 1142-7.

Loving the World by Carolyn Nystrom. God has created a glorious world. Our responsibility is to help preserve and protect it. From valuing the sanctity of life to sharing your faith to helping the oppressed to protecting the envi-ronment, these Bible studies will help you discover your role in God's crea-tion. 1143-5.

Pursuing Holiness by Carolyn Nystrom. Character traits such as honesty, self-control, sexual purity and integrity may seem out of date. Yet, God's will for us is that we live holy lives. Through Christ, we can find the strength we need to live in a way that glorifies God. These studies will help you to pursue the traits of holiness. 1147-8.

Staying Faithful by Andrea Sterk Louthan and Howard Louthan. This study guide is about wholehearted commitment to Christ. We will be motivated not only to persevere in Christ, but also to grow by taking the risks that will allow us to move forward in our Christian lives. Discover the power of faithfulness! 1146-X.